ON THE
Wings
of
SKY

ON THE Wings of SKY

Seemeen Khan Yousufzai
(SKY)

PARTRIDGE

Print information available on the last page.

To order additional copies of this book, contact
Toll Free 800 101 2657 (Singapore)
Toll Free 1 800 81 7340 (Malaysia)
orders.singapore@partridgepublishing.com

www.partridgepublishing.com/singapore

Contents

Survival

And so I Live...

Your acidic words,
Untasted by you,
Erode my heart,
But it knows to heal;
Your splintering stare,
Unseen by you,
Singes my soul,
But it knows to salve;
Your fatal hatred,
Unfelt by you,
Fragments my being,
But it knows to fuse;
And I do fly
For I know to mend,
And I do breathe
For I know to forego.
And so I live...

Seemeen Khan Yousufzai (SKY)

Ripples of Disturbia

Ripples of disturbia crashing against the shore of my fortress,
Forcing their way in, slamming against the door of my fastness.

I stand tall in the knowledge of my undeterred faith's steadfastness,
The sands of time have been cognizant of my voyage's vastness.

Trials of the past have polished my weak rough edges,
The smooth surface that I acquired is now for all ages.

Need I fear this oncoming wave, when I foresee myself reconquering?
Need I fear the pain of trials, when I foresee myself re-strengthening?

Shores of comfort until not lost,
Steps of valour unless not taken,
Wheels of motion until not turned,
The winds on the road of uncertainty,
Would not billow the cloud of my courage,
To sail through the storms of the ocean.

Ripples of disturbia crashing against the shore of my fortress,
Forcing their way in, slamming against the door of my fastness.

I stand tall in the knowledge of my undeterred faith's steadfastness,
The sands of time have been cognizant of my voyage's vastness...

You Smirk

You smirk when you hurt me
Thinking it is your words
That take power over me,
You leer when you cut me
Thinking it is your schemings
That got the better of me.

Yes, it hurt
Yes, it smarted
Yes, it got to me
But, you see not
It is I, who let it
It is I, who permitted it
It is I, who admitted
The pain to swamp my heart
The tears to sting my eyes
The stab to tremble my hand
For I loved you...

I got hurt
'Cause I loved
I got hurt
'Cause I cared
I got hurt
'Cause I crowned in my heart
One who was not worth the pain.

Seemeen Khan Yousufzai (SKY)

What you mistake as my defeat,
The pulsing love in my heart,
Shall soon overpower your cunning
By immersing you in its lake.

And with your heart made alive,
I shall see, then, the loud exhibit crying
Changing into silent tears of repent.

Sanguine Stance

I shed my tears in darkness,
The sable companion espoused my wounds,
Bequeathed with a friend who made no promise
Of a time when agony will let loose.

The silent camaraderie with the ebony
Had a lesson in it for me.

Across the turbulent fields I had trodden,
The momentary quietude offered a plain of cotton.
My sore feet splattered the whiteness with dotted signature,
The cotton softness and raven calm was for my thirst a full pitcher.

There forth began my novice romance
With a new chapter of sanguine stance.

Seemeen Khan Yousufzai (SKY)

Solitary Lioness

The zest in my veins
For a life of honour
Ya better toe the line
Or suffer, thereby.

I'll be your friend
I'll be your guide
You break the trust
And my wrath draws nigh.

You put me down
And I won't comply
I have lived
With my head held high.

Standing alone
On a plateau
The pride in my eyes
And dignity won't die.

A Solitary Lioness
Is what I may be
But with my ideals
I will travel far and fly.

Awakening the Mind

The Folly of Mankind

We write the sonnets of melody
In the song of life,
We paint the beads of merry
In the string of life.
We fail to see the painful truth
That follows life,
We fail to espy the beautiful lie
That is life.

We see not beyond the limited confines of earth,
We spare not even the deceased's final berth,
We garland those withered branches with daffodils of Wordsworth,
We shun the death, though it is what gives meaning to life's mirth.

Woe to the folly of mankind!
That diverts its attention
From its final destination
Yet speeding on the same road
Hoping to find a unique code
To eternal life; oh, it is so blind!

We scribe the tales of splendour
In the annals of life,
We weave the threads of wonder
In the pattern of life.

Seemeen Khan Yousufzai (SKY)

We fail to see the painful truth
That follows life,
We fail to espy the beautiful lie
That is life.

We live in a daze under the dazzles of showbiz lights,
We sell morals, creating hell in the hopes of utopian delights.
We adorn our artificial houses with plants grown without daylights,
We murder nature and create replicas
assuming we achieved new heights.

Woe to the folly of mankind,
That diverts its attention
From its final destination
Yet speeding on the same road
Hoping to find a unique code
To eternal life; oh, it is so blind!

Death at 0000 Hours

And they say there is peace in Death,
Yet, in the same breath, is a fear of Death,
And if there really be peace in Death,
Then, why do we endlessly dread you, Death?

If the end of all ends be in Death,
Why do we feel a new beginning in Death?
There is, in the graveyard, a lurking stillness of Death,
Is not that Silence heralding a storm following Death?

A treacherous thief they call you, Death,
Though, honest to your promise you are, Death.
Blamed you are for you cleverly catch them off-guard,
In this game of hide-and-seek, forever, taking the crown, Death.
Faultless you are, simply, skillful like the smoothness of sward
While varying your guise as a shape-shifting transporter, Death.

Oh hush...! They know not that you are but just an usher,
Escorting them to their seats, buckling for a climax on a roller-coaster,
An apocalyptic ride of utter cataclysms that follow you, Death.

Seemeen Khan Yousufzai (SKY)

Into the Dust

We sweat, bleed and toil,
For pleasures of a soft life,
Yet our final bed's dust.

We jiggle, juggle and joggle,
For comforts of a poised life,
Yet our final bed's dust.

We tweak, transform and refine,
For yesses from the elite fabric of life,
Yet our final bed's dust.

We seek, explore and wander,
For the harvest of blossoming hopes from life,
Yet our final bed's dust.

We build, collect and amass
For imprinting our mark in the spheres of life,
Yet our final bed's dust.

Thirsting life, we hasten towards dust,
Dreading life, we hasten towards dust,
Loving life, we hasten towards dust,
Mourning life, we hasten towards dust,
Life and us, pirouetting into the dust.

We live, love, laugh and cry,
For the realization of all spectra of life,
Yet our final bed's dust.

My Soul Becomes a Robin

All around me
Is this concrete kingdom,
Filled with casuistry,
That causes me misery.

The buildings around are concrete,
The hearts beating within them are concrete,
An outward varnish of civilization and morality.

Polished surfaces
That reflect an ominous darkness,
Steal away
From the glory of springtime promise.

Blinded by the mirage of beauty,
They pay no heed as I toll the bell
To awaken them to the deceit of their reality.

Forlorn, my soul begins to despair
Befuddled by appearances of actuality,
I start to trip, when...

Lo! there do I see,
Yonder's nature's kingdom,
Filled with innocence,
That infuses me with ecstasy.

14

Enthused with an alien joy,
My chest heaves,
My heart leaps.

My soul becomes a robin
And flies and sings,
With my chest bursting and heart bobbing,
Exuberantly I trill, heralding truth, on my new wings.

Seemeen Khan Yousufzai (SKY)

The Saga of a Sage

And the young child pouted,
Brows furrowing,
The candy he desired
Found home
In the hands of a sibling.
Upset with his parent
In a fit of childish temper,
He flung his poor,
Blameless sweet candy
Far away.
It tumbled until,
Lifelessly, it landed
Before the wooden walking stick
Of the humble hunched hoary man.

The child exclaimed,
"Oh, Father! See how bent
And crinkled that man is!"
The naive voice rang
Through the air,
Reaching the bent old man.
He looked up with his trembling head,
The neck too tired
To carry its weight.
He smiled a sad and wise smile,
His tired eyes
Holding wisdom unmatched.

Thus he relayed,
A saga of a sage,
"Young bud of life,
Once, there was a time
When my limbs were as supple as yours,
My skin as smooth as yours,
My heart as *vivo* as yours.

"My journey commenced
On meeting the fair maiden,
Called Life.
She enticed me
She invited me
To the wonders she had to offer.
I, curious and learning,
Grabbed at
And readily fell
For her allure.

"She made me love her,
She made me hate her,
She made me regret her,
She made me forget her,
Yet, she kept me
Wanting more of her.

"She made me see
The best of times
She gave me joy
With the loved ones I had
She filled me with expectations
And crushed them, mercilessly.

"She made me wonder
About who she was,
She made me wonder
Why she was,
She made me want to
Call it quits,
But, then,
Made me forget
All my sores,
With every new phase
That blossomed forth.

"Every new blossom
Brought along
A sad longing
For the times gone by.
Every new blossom,
Left behind
Trails on my skin
Of the paths trodden afore.

"But, young child,
The more I creased,
The more I straightened;
The more I ached,
The more I learned.

"My patience grew,
My wisdom bloomed
As my bones

Withered and waned,
And I learned
The value
Of each breathing moment.

"My bent shoulders
Carry a weight in bundles,
Dragged along the lines
Of my wizened face;
The weight of my years,
The weight of my wisdom,
The weight of my saying goodbyes,
The weight of my trove of delights,
The weight of valuing my Life's ration.

"So value what you get,
Young Spring of Life,
Let not your tomorrows
Beset with
Raw regrets."

Decadence

Entranced by the flutes of dazzle,
We are sucked into a cerebral state worn to a frazzle.
The voyage has been tricky to tackle,
Since man took from the forbidden apple.
There once was betwixt two sides a mighty tussle,
Who would fail, who would prevail, was a matter of much quarrel.
The land of weak soil gave way like the sands of time in grip
As man became overawed by the splendor and power of kingship.
We were created in the best of forms, for the best of deeds
We reduced ourselves to the worst of deeds,
to attain the best of forms, no heeds.
Mankind lost its identity in the gamble of power,
Its hold over the rope of reason loosened in the tug of war.
The clouds of darkness and misery are looming over us
Lost, with decaying courage, we merely look
up and await its rage upon us.
Grief takes deep blood-rich fulfilling breaths,
As atrocities rise the count of wrongful and unjust deaths.
Yet, that position of high esteem still awaits us,
If only we would muster the courage to rise
up from this quagmire of puss.

They Experiment With Life

And they think they are in control,
Their limited minds, do not know soon they'll lose it all.
They snatch an infant from the mother's protective lap,
Seeking to create innovative work borne out of someone's mishap.
They play like a cruel thoughtless child,
That tortures and kills an insect to explore the side of wild.
They extinguish the burning flame of life one too many times,
No living kingdom has been spared from their heartless crimes.
To gain name and fame their diabolical deeds
of destruction pave paths of death,
Here's a task for these experimenters, why not bring
one back to life or supply with a single breath?
So, before you experiment with life speeding it towards night,
Know that you haven't been blessed with intellect
enough to bring it back to light!

Seemeen Khan Yousufzai (SKY)

The Rise From Ashes:
A Tale Of One Country

Let me tell you a story,
Let me tell you a tale,
It is all but true,
It is old, but will be told anew,
Of people made of flesh and bone
Like you and I,
Of people, who fought for their throne,
On whom you could rely.

Rising from the flowing bloodstream,
An ocean of courage, zest and bravery,
Bobbing with the hope of a new spring
That would blossom their buds to openly sing
In a land that they will call their own,
In a land where they have an identity of their own
In a land where they are free to:
Practise their beliefs
Enlighten their minds
Advance their progress
And give back to the identity they achieved
And carry forth the heritage they received
From those who sacrificed all and breathed
Of air that ringed with freedom and pride perceived.

And they gathered under a flag as one,
With honour and life running in their blood as one,
They were now a force to be reckoned with like no other, my son
It was their unity that held them through what had begun.

Let me tell you a story,
Let me tell you a tale,
It is all but true,
It is not old, and is well-known to you,
Of people made of flesh and bone
Like you and I,
Of people who have left us to moan,
On whom you could never rely.

Growing in the flowing bloodstream,
An ocean of deceit, wile and yellow-belly,
Bouncing with the jangle of looting
Taken from the vaults of our nation, leaving nothing,
From a land that they call their own;
From a land that gave them an identity of their own;
From a land where they foster:
Creating rifts among the people,
Subjugating the minds of the people,
Hurdling the progress of the people,
Maligning the sanctity of the identity they were granted,
Discarding the heritage of sacrifice, wholly recanted
Ideologies promoting honesty, caught oft-
times in disgrace red-handed,
Where is the freedom, where is the pride, they are all but stranded...

Seemeen Khan Yousufzai (SKY)

And now we gather under different flags, never as one,
The friction between honour and life is eroding all as one,
When the system is reeked with corruption, such that none can shun,
Promises to undo it all are heard, if only less
was said and more was done!

Yet, the hope of a new spring
That would blossom our buds to openly sing
Not just of their soaring past, but the present's elevating wing,
And to the future, you will then
Tell them a story,
Tell them a tale,
It will all be but true,
It will be new, but reminiscent of a past view,
Of people made of flesh and bone,
Like you and I,
Of people who would restore our throne,
And revive our trust, by and by.

Reassembling from the flowing bloodstream
A hightide of grit, spunk and bruised self-esteem,
That would make their fire fierier than a dragon's fire,
Sparkling the glory of the nation, bringing their passion to boil,
While their bruises would sting and burn them as they heal,
It would also be the force to ignite their drive to turn their dreams real,
They will regain their lost strength to regain their:
Rights to embrace their deen,
Spark their minds' lanterns,
March towards their long-due progress,
And give back to the identity they had achieved,
And carry forth the forgotten heritage they had received,
From those who had sacrificed all and had breathed
Of air that ringed with freedom and pride, perceived.

And they would re-gather under the flag as one,
Once again, with honour and life running in their blood as one,
They will be a force to be reckoned with like no other, my son
It will, again, be their unity that would hold
them through what had begun.

Oh, and how I wish to live that moment
That would create a history for eons to come,
And tell them a story
Of hope and faith,
And tell them a tale
Of what was once lost, was then regained.

Out of
the Past

In The Walk of a Past Life

In the rains of the storm,
In the silence of my solitude,
I walk again on the paths
I once long back traversed.

In the walk of a past life
Every step I take forth
Fear shivers and harshly pulls me back
'Don't venture there!' says the silent foe.

I reply, holding its hand firmly,
'It is time we pay our due.'
And march ahead, sturdily.

In the walk of the past life
I meet strangers by every stride
In the walk of the past life
I sense I know'em from beyond the bay.

I come across Denial
Who greets me like an old friend,
With a dip in the river of numbness
I am washed away.

Seemeen Khan Yousufzai (SKY)

I come across Trauma
Who greets me like an old friend,
With thunders of pain, terror and helplessness
I am seared ash grey.

I come across Grief
Who greets me like an old friend,
With a reminder of wretchedness
I am morphed into emotional decay.

I come across Anger
Who greets me like an old friend,
With a memento of blame and bitterness
I am, again, led astray.

In the crowd of old friends
My fidgety eyes look for
A familiar face on this familiar path
A lost soul, the sole reminder of myself that I hath.

In the massiveness of the night
With the butchering of my mind
I walk again with a new thought
I wonder what the night has in store.

Fear has resigned
Curiosity has overtaken
My being breathes in the familiar torture
It savours the sweetness of the inverse future.

In the walk of the past life,
The fiery wounds await me
In the walk of the past life,
I have set out to dress the lesions.

I come across my Child-Self
Who greets me with a lost look,
With a pain that gashes through my being
I am blown away.

I come across my Child-Self
And I cease to exist...alone.

I come across my Child-Self
And I form a bond becoming...a bone.

Oh! Drop all the promises of not breaking down,
Drop all the facade, I don't want indestructibility's crown.

Let me cry
Let me weep
Let me hold my Child-Self
In an embrace and sleep.

Let us pour forth the pain in our chests,
Let us rub our eyes in our thorn-nests,
Let the flow wash away the stabbing broken glasses and the rest.

In the walk of the past life,
My old-self tells my child-self
I wish I was there with you when no one was,

Seemeen Khan Yousufzai (SKY)

In the walk of the past life,
My old-self tells my child-self
I wish I was there to protect you when no one was

In the walk of the past life,
My old-self tells my child-self
I wish was there to stand for you when no one was.

In the walk of the past life,
My old-self tells my child-self,
I wish I could wipe your tears and hold you tight when no one did

In the walk of the past life,
My old-self tells my child-self
I wish I could hide you from all the evil in this world
You had to witness.
You had to endure.

In the walk of the past life,
My old-self tells my child-self
I wish I was there for you...

My child-self looks at me
With a look wise beyond its years
'Don't let the cruelty of the world
Crumble the purity of your soul,
You have to collide with circumstances,
But keep yourself whole.'

I get up, enlightened
Walking towards the morning
Taking tentative steps forward.

Every inch I move forward
The skeletal hand of the past
Clutches at my robes and pulls me backward.

I hear this wise companion warning me,
'O, my shadow of times ahead,
Let not the root of despair grow a tree
It is time for you to live for yourself and for me.'

Seemeen Khan Yousufzai (SKY)

Halt, Oh Sands of Time

Halt! Oh sands of time,
Halt and flow back!

Your coarse texture thwarts me
From pouring forth freely,
Summoning me to repair my time
Bidding me to relive like a child...

Oh sands of time, halt and flow back!
Let me meet myself,
Let me breathe with myself,
Let me free myself...

Let me sprinkle tinkling childish laughter
In the lines of my palm,
Let me unwrinkle the creases of worry
From the plain of my brow...

Let me unchain the restrains of inhibition
From the mounting pain in my heart,
Let me rein in the shadows of fear
From the walls of my mind...

Let me pluck the stinging bruising thorns
Accompanying the isolated gestures
Of sham care and affection
From the skin of my trust...

Let all these anomalies flow in these tears
While I write this missive of appeal to you,
For it may smoothen the coarseness
Of the sands of my time...

Thus, without the rough glitches,
I shall merge with you
In soul and mind and body
And will slip and flow with you.

But, 'til then, halt!
Halt and flow back, oh sands of my time...

Seemeen Khan Yousufzai (SKY)

Planting the Beads of Light

One day,
I was given
An unblemished and flawless
Sacred pearl necklace.

One day,
I wore it,
Its magnificence and luxuriousness
Made me breathless.

One day,
I ventured out,
Its allure and richness
Turned all avaricious.

One day,
They tore it,
The exposed and defenseless
Rope of weakness.

Oh!
I was in distress!
I felt so helpless.
Had I been reckless?

I tried to save them
'Fore they hit the ground
But
They proved swifter
And flowed in a scattered shower of stream.

Pieces of my heart
Accompanied them
When
They struck the ground
Amidst the surrounding petrifying cachinnation.

I got down on all fours
On the ground
Then
Began collecting
The scattered, dust-bathed queenly orbs of light.

My tears washed
The smut-enveloped pearls
And
I saw traces of a spectrum of colours
Peeking through the curtains of grime.

Ah!
The fireflies of mirth
Rekindle the hearth
And revivify my earth.

Today,
I stop here,
In the deserted street so narrow
Gauging the meads of blight.

Today,
I mark here,
In the sight window of a crossbow
Slicing the weeds of spite.

Today,
I wait here,
In the hope of a new morrow
Overcoming the shadows of night.

Today,
I sit here,
In the string of sorrow
Planting the beads of light.
Planting the beads of light.

Hope

and

Disquiet

The Canvas of My Future Kingdom

Buzzing, bustling, cackling
Knocking at the locked chamber
The voices that try to sear through
The blissful peace of my mind.

Gazing, looking, viewing
Staring at some empty space
My eyes let in the senseless images
Of the surrounding commotion.

Thinking, dreaming, planning
Sketching a beautiful vista of wishes
My mind vibrantly paints and weaves
The canvas of my future kingdom.

Rising Disquiet

I packed my scars of the past under the guise of a new skin,
And I bore the recurrent smothering of the darkness and
gloom in the hopes of ringing a new freedom in.

I learned to smile and laugh, to breathe every moment of life,
And I cherished the littlest things that
encompass a world of their own light.

Yet, I saw the approaching engulfing darkness in
the clouds always hovering over my porch,
And I felt something cracking, something breaking,
something snuffing in my lonely soul's torch.

Thus, again, I wrapped my shawl of bruises around my heart,
And I braced myself for the brittle winter harshness's start.

Expectant Eyes

She braces herself for the oncoming winter blusters
Wrapping her shawl of grief over her shoulders

She foresees a barren landscape awaiting her on her course
The higher the expectations the tougher the path's force

Thus, the sun sets in her expectant eyes,
While, her heart rebels and brazenly denies...

Seemeen Khan Yousufzai (SKY)

Looming Fear

I run miles and miles away from fear,
I glance over my shoulder and find nothing there...

I stand still and frozen from fear,
Feet rooted and covered in concrete too austere...

I feel a cloud approaching of dread so sheer,
Blanketing me, chasms of emptiness in front of concrete feet appear...

I discern the nebulous shape of fear,
If I allow it to become precise, I disappear...

Haiku

Through The Looking Glass (Haiku)

Through the looking glass,
I see, pick, and re-arrange
The shattered pieces.

Seemeen Khan Yousufzai (SKY)

Friend to Foe (Haiku)

Silence stayed staunch, while
The friend, watched my dust turn to
Ashes, like a foe.

Changing Faces (Haiku)

I blink my eyes and
Seasons change, faces more oft,
Few are veils, mostly masks.

Seemeen Khan Yousufzai (SKY)

Memories (Haiku)

What were eons far,
Shape into concrete forms when
opens mind's treasure.

Conjoined Twins (Haiku)

Takes an instant for
Hate's thunderous dark clouds to
Cover love's sunlight.

Relics Of Romanticism

A Twilight Adieu

Across the lake,
In the sea of sands
A soothing lazy breeze
Plays with a sandy-hued lock of hair
That has an independent spirit of its own.

Away from the rest of its clan
It dances wildly
Like a sensual gypsy dancer
Its wild freedom
Obstructing the line of vision
Of the intense deep eyes,
That encompasses a lost world within its realm.

Scrutinising the message of nature
Encoded in the ambience
Under the canopy of the firmament
The amber-gold-rayed brown eyes breathe in
The change in the sky as twilight approaches.

And the sun winks at the eyes
Through the clouds
As a final goodbye for the day
And the eyes crinkle at the corners
Lighting up as the sun lights up the sky,
Thus, the silent watchers
Bid each other a sweet adieu.

Seemeen Khan Yousufzai (SKY)

Once Upon a Moonlit Night

Under the sleepy starry skies
Under the thousand drowsy eyes
The moon standing tall and wise
Ushering in morrow, saying goodbyes
A hundred thousand questions arise
In the deepest chamber where heart lies
As the wandering gypsy music dies...

What is it, young heart?
What is it that you seek?

After a hard day's labour
Do you seek the comfort of silk covered pillows?
Or the warmth of the loving lap of a fellow's?

After treading a path of thorns
Do you seek the lure and shine of a terrain of gold-laden mass?
Or the coolness of a patch of green grass?

Amidst the life on earth so still,
Amidst the deep sighs that trill,
The night celebrates twinkling life at will
Guiding the morrow, like a beacon on the hill
In the cave where wild thoughts mill,
A hundred thousand questions more brim, until
The eyes behold the heavens beyond the window-sill...

What is it young heart?
What is it that you thirst for?

For an evening of leisure
Do your senses thirst for the coalesence of red wine and red eyes?
Or the fragrant intoxication of red roses
relating fables the young heart vies?

For a life that is fulfilled,
Would you acquire pricey pearls by millions from a falling leaf?
Or gather in palms priceless tears borne of love and grief?

While the moon intoxicates the nightly skies,
While the moon awaits the fiery sun to rise,
Standing lonely shedding her grief in dewy cries,
Longing for him, who'll bathe an army in its orange flamy fires,
The young heart, restless and curious, questions its desires
As the moon's reflection shudders in fear in the lake of croaking spies,
Announcing her loss, as the sun chooses regality, ceding all ties...

Seemeen Khan Yousufzai (SKY)

Towards the Rising Sun

After
A nightly battle
Rising mighty and proud,
Brilliantly blazing the skies,
With open arms, here we welcome
The shining knight of light.
Towards the rising sun,
Here we come.

To Serenity

I hear a crow cawing
Somewhere farther away
My eyes scan the scene
And there swoops in
The grey-black murder
Of three crows.

They latch onto
Different perches,
Away from one another, and me,
With solitary silent stares
Looking Into the space ahead,
Like me.

No, they do not
Come with a bad omen
Instead seem to have
Fallen a victim
To the strong daze
Of serenity that binds the place.

What is in the air:
An invisible spell,
A gaseous drug,
Or, just the cure for
The restless, perturbed heart,
That transfixes every soul?

59

Seemeen Khan Yousufzai (SKY)

The world is quiet,
The world is at peace,
The word chaos exists not,
As my raven companions
And I, breathe in
The fresh peace.

There, my soul latches onto
The molecules of serenity
In the still air
As if we were made
Of the same substance,
Bound by the force of cohesion.

Pure Pulchritude

The pureness of her beauty lies in the modesty of her eyes,
The pureness of her beauty lies in her unpretentious gaze,
The pureness of her beauty lies in her coy smile.

Her smile speaks sweet dreams of vast multitude,
Her eyes hold everlasting hopes of great magnitude,
Her air radiates affable allure of deep pulchritude...

Seemeen Khan Yousufzai (SKY)

Hide and Seek

Rustling in the trees,
The teasing sun's comradeship,
With the windy clouds.

This celestial tease,
Leaves me puffing for cool breeze
Playing hide and seek.

The
Aching Soul

Sitting here all alone...

Sitting here all alone...
The clock ticks
In reply
To my pained heartbeats...

My heart aches,
My mind is restive,
Whilst I discern
A shape in the misty haze
Of a distant past.
As it moves like a whisper
I sense the danger
This is not a stranger.

I know it...
My mind knows it...

It is an acquaintance of old
That reappears
From time to time
With a vengeance...

...Ensnares us.
Entangles us.
Combats us.
Afflicts us.
Torments us.
For forgetting it
Since the last we met.

Slowly sneaking.
Slowly spreading.
Slowly swamping.
Slowly striking.
Slowly slaughtering.
My mind submits to it.
And I submit to it.

But, neither do I know,
Nor does my mind know,
How to compel my heart
To submit to it.
Submit to this spate.
Succumb to this plague.

Thus,
My heart flutters
In its fitful, unyielding state,
Bruising itself
In a hopeless attempt to escape
The embrace of spiked pain;
The cage of barbed chains.

Thus,
My heart whimpers
And sheds tears of blood
While it painfully beats
In reply
To the ticks of the clock
As I sit here, all alone...

Sing Me A Last Lullaby

Don't rush forth, O Moon,
My heart's rhythm flutters
Not knowing what morrow utters.

Don't rush forth, O Moon,
My heartbeat stops
As the dread of the expected knocks.

Don't rush forth, O Moon,
For you may be rushing forth to view
The death of our heart's desires, bidding them adieu.

Don't rush forth, O Moon,
Stay with me, be my harmony
Why not linger in each other's company?

Don't rush forth, O Moon,
Hold me in your silver arms' tomb,
Let your rays be an ointment to my wounds.

Don't rush forth, O Moon,
But, if you must, take me to your realm's quiet,
Sing me a last lullaby, lull me to sleep tonight.

The

Healing Soul

Ode to the Wild Blue Rose

While your red mate
Steals the rosy show,
Dancing in its glory
Of evoking love
In barren hearts,
Fusing its colour
In lives around,
You, Wild Blue Rose,
Drifted and chose
A life so vice versa
Sucking the poison,
Drinking the venom
From the lives around;
Suffering in silence,
Standing in solitude,
Shrouded in mystery,
An unsung hero,
Ousted long ago
With undying sorrow,
Wounded blue by love's arrow,
On whose cheek glows
Tears as the night dew flows,
The Blue Rose wildly grows.

Seemeen Khan Yousufzai (SKY)

Ode to a Healing Soul

Wounded souls silently live in the pain
Waiting for a prayer that will assuage their mane

Providing a solace for the throat with blood stain,
Cut through with the silent screamings' echoes' train

The caressing dull glow of the crepuscule's gain
Affects the bruised one to writhe in fires of bane

In the night's soothing embrace, the embers wane;
Exuviating, the skin breathes fresh, within a new reign.

Spiritual Odyssey

The Revival

Centuries ago mankind's heart turned cold,
Centuries ago mankind's belief was sold.
When the Mercy of God was bestowed on them
They buried their faces and the Mercy alive, 'cept some.
The damsels whose adornment was their sparkling modesty,
Let the wild animals pierce through the veil to reveal naked vanity.
Centuries ago when the voice of reason was a long forgotten echo,
And the walls of faith were nothing more than a crumbled ghetto,
Did arrive a Knight in plain clothes with a simple message
To revitalize the fossils of faith of what had become a wreckage.

His blood coursed through the streets to invigorate their reason,
A great amount of toil and sweat were invested
through numerous seasons.
The Mercy of God was allowed her right to flourish,
Her nubile form was once more covered for modesty to nourish.
At long last, did they see the light of truth,
Giving hope to generations and generations of youth.

Centuries hence, mankind's heart has turned cold,
Centuries hence, mankind's belief has been sold.
When the Mercy of God is bestowed on them,
They scrape and bury it before its shape has wholly become.
The maiden and the mistress are both undressed,
The veilsome are jeered at and called supressed.

Seemeen Khan Yousufzai (SKY)

Centuries hence, when the voice of reason is a distant echo,
And the walls of faith are eroding into a crumbled ghetto,
Do we await the arrival of the Knight's progeny,
To revitalize the fossils of faith to smoothen out this timely anomaly.

Seeking the Light

Through the alleys of life,
I gathered, embraced, and absorbed
The shiny dust on my self, heart, and conscience.

Springing lively to my needs
On the cobblestones of whims and fancies,
I tripped once while hopping from one to another.

Trudging through the tundra plains,
I pondered on the fickleness of my wants...
Whence I received the valued glitter yesterday,
today mattered no more.

Coursing through the snaking darkness,
My soul searched for a source of permanent light,
Thence, I came across the majesty of the
place of worship and repentance.

Flying through space,
The innate fondness of the moth for natural light
That it sought, could not be snuffed by the allurement of street lights.

Thus, in repentance,
I bowed down my head while rising in pudicity, I implored,
'Wash away from my heart, this world's bright
dust, replacing it with Your Touch.'

Seemeen Khan Yousufzai (SKY)

And He is The One

I recreate myself in the struggle to survive,
But what doesn't change is You.
I destroy myself to metamorphosize,
But what remains of me is You.

My eyes remained dry in pain,
Some called me strong, others a frost;
They saw not my unseen tears of bane,
But upon You Alone it was not lost.

My existence carried no weight,
An unnoticeable being swarmed by hate;
A silent drop in a deafening sea,
Yet, You Alone could discern me.

I have used countless disguises
To cover the bruises from every fall,
My faults and flaws in different sizes
Though, You Alone see through all.

You See me more than I see me,
You Know me more than I know me,
You Hear me more than I hear me,
You, Al-Baseer ul-Aleem us-Samee'.

I lose myself in this mad world's reins,
I remain not with me, He remains with me,
I am unforgiving of me, His Forgiveness overcomes me,
So I rise to reap the next world's gains.

My Lord, Knower of the unknown,
From Whom not an atom's weight is hidden,
My Creator, Who knows all that has ever risen,
He is the Most Kind, the Omniscient, the Well-Known!

Seemeen Khan Yousufzai (SKY)

The Golden Virtue

And what has long befallen me
Will reach its timely death
And patience is the golden virtue
That I must hold onto every breath.

It is surely a long long road
Of trials and tribulations
Of sorrows and afflictions
But the fruit is well worth the thorns' pricks.

For God is with those who have patience
Thus, I'll seek help through it and prayers
And when my hand grasps and plucks the long due fruit
The stinging pain will be but a distant memory.

The Raging Remorse

Woe is me, for I have sinned and sinned,
Woe is me, for I have suffered and suffered,
The glaring self-reproach that I bear,
The glaring misdeeds that I now doubly fear,
Are transcribed in bold in my book of deeds,
As much as I religiously blot them out,
Pushing back their recurrent memories
They surface oft times.

As I prostrate, I see a stereoscopy of my sins,
Orbitting in front of my eyes
Like a merry-go-round,
Evoking images of my death bed,
Of what will pass before my eyes,
Before death befriends me.

Lord of the worlds!
I sacrificed the tranquility of my heart,
With my wilful trespassing,
So blinded by the nothingness around,
So led astray by the emptiness within,
I could not see what I knew so well.

Thoughts of backspacing moments
Run through my desperate heart,
My restless conscience
Tosses and turnes in its guilty bed,

Which it ambitiously made for itself,
In a bid to sedate itself.

I gambled with life, to bear losses,
Yet in the losses lie an unusual gain,
A perspective so profound, that humbles me,
That halts me from being
Too quick to judge,
Too quick to label,
Too quick to give up
On those around.

Verily, the burden of my heart,
Will weigh me down
'Til I gasp my last breath,
Yet, this heart will remain hopeful,
Wishing for its prayers and repentance,
To be accepted.

Hitherto, the burden of my heart,
Will be carried forth,
'Til I gasp my last breath,
With the shining ray of hope
That thus far I possess not the vice
Of being unconscious to all vice.

Printed in the United States
By Bookmasters